DONNA ASHWORTH

Words to live by

A DAILY JOURNAL

Write your way to clarity and calm

First published in the UK in 2024 by Black & White Publishing

An imprint of Bonnier Books UK

4th Floor, Victoria House, Bloomsbury Square, London, WC1B 4DA

Owned by Bonnier Books, Sveavägen 56, Stockholm, Sweden

Hardback ISBN: 978-1-78530-715-7

A CIP catalogue record for this book is available from the British Library.
Typeset by Nic&Lou
Printed and bound in Latvia

1 3 5 7 9 10 8 6 4 2

Black & White Publishing is an imprint of Bonnier Books UK

www.bonnierbooks.co.uk

A year of discovery and writing for

This year I want to feel more

On difficult days I'll remind myself

I want to look back on this year and see how I

I don't write because I am sunshine in human form
I write to bring in light and save the dark from taking over
that war must always be managed — it's never won
but it's never, EVER, lost either
and that is enough

because whilst my bleeding heart has suffered along the way
it also feels such beauty. And feels it so deeply that the
joy of it can feel like pain

and I've learned to love that too
just like I've learned to love myself for all the things
they told me to change.

Introduction

I don't write because I am brimming with sunshine. I write because I naturally run dark.

And those of us who run dark, who feel hard, who see everything, must daily work at that disposition in order to enjoy this life – to survive this world.

I write to encourage an attitude of gratitude. To remind myself that living with kindness as my lead changes everything, quite like magic. And if there is magic in this life, that is surely it.

I write to combat a mind full of chaotic thoughts flying in myriad directions. Like pulling a thread through the eye of a needle and into cloth, these words can be stitched into a picture that makes sense.

I write to remind myself that the only way, the *only way*, to combat the losses of this life is to love harder. And by reminding myself, it seems to remind you too.

For some time now I have wanted to create a place we could do this together. And here she is. A safe space to kick-start your writing again or – perhaps the bravest step of all – to begin.

If you take to this practice and find your flow, maybe you can share some of your pages with me and with all of us on social media? Let's see. One day at a time . . . and this is first and foremostly for *you*. An act of true self-care . . .

When I say *happy new year*
I'm really wishing you
more happy days
than sad days
more joy than misery
more laughter than tears
more bravery than fear

and the wisdom to accept
that they all belong.

From 'Happy New Year', *To the Women*

HOW TO JOURNAL WITH ME

Some time ago I began using focus words at the start of a new year, to replace the punishing tradition of resolutions. On social media I have been allocating readers a word each January, and I thought we could carry that over here.

A focus word does not rule out all the other ways we can grow; it simply gives an anchor when overwhelm or chaos hits. I have recently had 'hope', 'brave', 'faith/trust', and each of these brought me so much. Bringing the word to the forefront of your mind acts much like mindfulness and meditation. It can also spark new perspectives and lots of introspection.

So, I thought, why not have a word each month (as well as one for the year)? You can pick your own or join in with my suggestions. How to choose? If it feels like your word (or sometimes if it really does NOT feel like your word), then your instinct is telling you what you need. I like to flow with nature all year round, simply because facing against the wind takes far too much precious energy.

These words will help you put pen to paper when inspiration is absent and keep the flow flowing.

And on we go . . .

I have pulled together my favourite focus words for you to choose from or to inspire your own. Pay attention to how each word makes you feel as you say it out loud. If none of the words resonate fully, close your eyes and choose at random, let the book magic decide.

Faith

Trust

Charity

Kindness

Light

Grace

Brave

Truth

Energy

Serenity

New

Authenticity

Passion

Simplicity

Joy   Peace

                    Contentment

                                          Creativity

Home

            Courage   Clarity

Excitement   Curiosity

            Embrace

                              Dream

Spiritual   Free

            Awake

                              Accept

Wonder   Health

I am often asked how or why I began to write, and the most simple answer is that I always have. Words feel like numbers to me in that putting them together in the correct format can unlock many doors in my mind and heart. When my feelings are raw and destructive, placing them on paper takes the edge off their sharp corners. When worries and to-dos overwhelm, writing them down shines light on the parts that are exaggerated by ego. It helps me prioritise what is truly important and what is driven by perfectionism. Drawing down the words that fly around my head like circling birds creates order from chaos. And it helps me peek behind the curtain when I am hiding truths even from myself.

We are all creative, and if you haven't found your thing of choice yet, the fact you have this book in your hands tells me that journalling is for you. Just begin. There is no judgement when creativity abounds, and removing the need to be 'good' at something is like taking your foot off a hose pipe: the flow will let go.

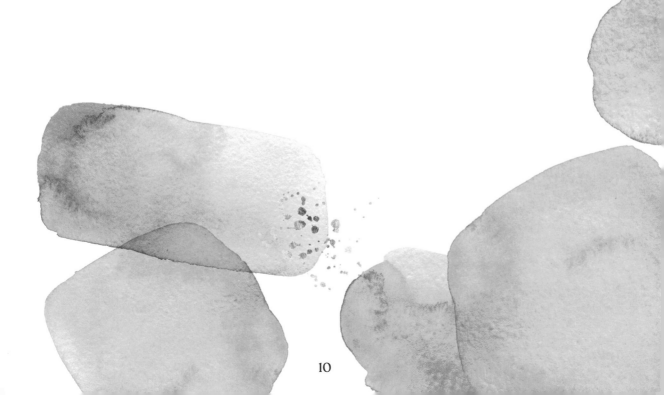

TAKE THE PEN

I don't remember when it happened
the day I realised I couldn't please everyone after all
the day it sunk in that no one can truly do that

if I could remember the day exactly, I would celebrate it
every year
like a birthday or a wedding
because that was the day I really started to live
the day I gave myself a gift

we are not here for a long time, my friends, so if you are living
to please, living to pander, living to 'fit in', you are wasting
those precious grains of sand that swiftly fall through the hole

your journey is not the same as those who went before you
you do not have to follow a path or fulfil an expectation
your story should be written by you, never for you

take the pen
type the words
turn the page
open your mind and let your imagination build your future

for you

if this chapter isn't bringing you joy
rewrite it
it's your book.

From *The Right Words*

USE THIS SPACE

to explore your thoughts and feelings about being a writer

REGENERATE

The festive season is a sensory overload for all. We are spent and depleted, despite the joy and fun. I have never believed January to be the time for new, the time to rearrange yourself into something more palatable for the world. Rather I have always felt January was the calm after the storm. A time to rest, recoup and regenerate. Let your mind have no fixed thoughts of all you should and must be doing; instead, make the most of the minutiae around you and be mindful of all the tasks that fight falsely for your attention. There is time. You are not in a rush to be a whole new you, not while Mother Nature clearly signals you otherwise. Prioritise what must be done. And as for any moments you have to play with as you like, be brave enough to rest. Resting is doing. And it is vital. By the end of this month you will better know what changes you really do wish to make. Let it unfurl as it will. Ignore the shouts from society about 'a better you' and 'a whole new me' . . . hold your patience. Your time to rise will come soon.

Adapted from *Growing Brave*

January

Why start another year gifted to us on this earth with demands on our already overstrained humanity, when we could be learning to accept we were always supposed to be imperfect? This is where the beauty lives. And if we could only find that beauty, we would also find peace.

WELCOME IN, JANUARY

A month of rest and regeneration. Now is not the time to rise. It is the month I use to slow down and reflect on what I want to focus on for the rest of the year. What would it help you to focus on? If you haven't already, take a moment now to choose a word to guide you this month, one that will help you find purpose this year. Words I think about in January include rest, reconnection, regeneration, respite and solace. To help you get into the habit of writing regularly, start by reflecting on a different question every day. Try to keep returning to your guiding word of the month. There are prompts to help you, if you find them useful.

My word for the month is

I hope this word will bring in

17

Day 1

What is making you feel hopeful right now?

Day 2

How is your guiding word helping you?

Day 3

How do you feel about yourself as a writer?

Day 4

Look around you and write about something you noticed

Day 5

What has been on your heart recently?

Day 6

Write about the weather and how it makes you feel

Day 7

What are you proud of yourself for lately?

Reflections

On days when your creativity is flowing freely, elaborate on a thought, a journal question or a day-to-day happening here. If you find you have nothing to say in this moment, come back to this space when you do (and you will).

Shine light into the dark corners
of your mind
take a good look
at the scary parts
you are afraid to enter into
they are quite different
once that light is on them
they cannot hold any power over you
in the burning glare of your shine.

From 'Shadows', *Wild Hope*

Day 8

If today were an emotion, I would call it _____ because

Day 9

As January has progressed, how is your energy?

Day 10

The critical thoughts that keep showing up are

Day 11

I thought about my guiding word recently when ...

Day 12

What weighs most heavily on your mind?

Day 13

If you could change one thing within your control,
what would it be? Why have you not changed it?

Day 14

What are your reflections on how your guiding word(s) could
help when you react to or struggle with something?

Reflections

Why not use this space to list the things you feel may be holding you back, weighing you down or stopping your flow? As you write them out, try to identify which emotions are real and valid and which fears and worries could be products of anxiety, stress or comparison. How could you flip the perspective?

Joy sneaks in
as you pour a cup of coffee
watching the sunlight
hit your favourite tree
just right.

From 'Joy Chose You', *Wild Hope*

Day 15

Describe what you slowed down to think about lately

Day 16

How are you including your inner child?

Day 17

What do you notice about your thoughts when
you try to slow down?

Day 18

Which limitations stop you from fully feeling peaceful?

Day 19

Where does your attention normally go?

Day 20

January is often a month of new beginnings.
What would you like to start?

Day 21

Write about a time you felt a strong emotion. Was it hiding another emotion? Was it made of fear? Invite it in again to find out more

Reflections

How are you feeling? Have you been able to slow down a little and take some extra moments to still your mind and think about yourself? How has your guiding word for January helped? As we nudge towards the end of the month, I would like to invite you to look for moments of rest, calm and reflection in your day, no matter how busy you are. Remember that the time and mental space you can create to recharge in January will give you energy and courage for the rest of the year.

You're not here to burn out
you're here to burn brightly
protect that precious light of yours
you only get one.

From 'Mother Nature Wants a Word', *Life*

Day 22

Spend some time bringing awareness to your body
and write about how it feels

Day 23

Write down five true things about yourself

Day 24

Remind two important people in your life how much they mean to you. What happened?

Day 25

When you are sad, how do you process it?

Day 26

Write down five things you are grateful for

Day 27

Write down five true things about your January so far

Day 28

Spend time observing something ordinary, then write
a freestyle short poem

PROMPT: Magic appears in everyday moments. Such wonder is found in the small

BECOMING

You are always becoming
the person you were born to be
before the world began to mould you
to its pattern
and not your own
you are always becoming
she who learned to hide
and shape-shift
to suit the crowd
the mood
the room
you are always becoming
and every time you release
a little more of her
to the world
I like to think Mother Nature
breathes out
exhales
a little more deeply . . .
here she is . . .
keep becoming
keep becoming.

From *I Wish I Knew*

Day 29

When you are rested, how do you feel?

Day 30

Write down three things that bring you joy

Day 31

If there is one thing you would like to work towards changing
this year, what would it be and why?

Reflections

As January bids us farewell, take a few moments to reflect on how you feel. How easy are you finding it creating time to write and reflect? Do you judge yourself for missing days or not being perfect? Remember, we are here to let go of the foot on the hose pipe and that judgement will turn off the tap entirely. Read back through your daily entries and use the space below to write about your thoughts and experiences.

LIFE BEGINS

Life begins the day you decide
that it does
the day you realise
that each day you open your eyes
and take a breath
is another day you have been gifted
on this planet

From 'Life Begins', *Life*

February

I wish I knew a lifetime ago
that no matter how much of the world I scoured
I would not find a better garden
than the one I could grow myself
if only I knew how.

From 'I Wish I Knew', *I Wish I Knew*

FEBRUARY

To me, February is a springboard, a step up to light. A short and snappy month that passes in the blink of an eye compared to the tortoise-like trundle of January. If January is the hardest month of the year, then February is most definitely its laid-back sister. Neither here nor there in essence, but always reassuring in its solidarity and so very much kinder. February sees the collective relaxing of the world's resolutions and punitive measures and could surely be heralded as the month we accept the old us back into the fold. If you have been flowing with me through January, you may have avoided the 'old me–new me' wave, but if not, welcome back to accepting yourself just as you are. Now that you have, it could be time to start pinning things you would like to change within your world to the fabric of the universe. We have plenty of time.

FEBRUARY

My word for the month is

I hope this word will allow me to

Day 1

What thoughts have been at the forefront of
your mind recently?

Day 2

When do you find it most useful to use your focus word?

Day 3

How do you feel about yourself right now?

Day 4

What feels different this month compared to last?

Day 5

What is the hardest thing about your day?
Could a fresh perspective help ease it?

Day 6

Which emotions are you feeling at the moment?

Day 7

What have you done for self-care recently?

Reflections

Use this space to set some gentle intentions for yourself now that the year is in flow and January has passed. Which habits are holding you down? Could you work on releasing some stuck emotions or perhaps allocate more fun or travel into your life? Would you like to focus on prioritising friendships or a hobby? Jot your thoughts down freely; this is merely food for thought at the moment. We still have time . . .

I think, the secret of life
is to laugh when you must
and cry when you should
and let everything else come and go.

From 'Life', *Life*

Day 8

If today were a colour, what would it be and why?

Day 9

How are your energy levels this month and how could
you best increase that flow?

Day 10

When overwhelm increases, how do you feel and how
do you push it back?

Day 11

Write down five true things about your February so far

Day 12

Have you noticed your negative thinking increasing
or decreasing since starting this journal?

Day 13

What made you laugh recently and have you laughed often?

Day 14

Write down five ways in which you are worthy from the point of view of your fiercest admirer

Reflections

I would love you to use this space to write about your favourite happening from the past weeks. Why was this moment special and worth remembering? Could you welcome in more of these occasions and encourage the same feelings?

Joy is *supposed* to slither through the cracks of your imperfect life that's how joy *works*.

From 'Joy Chose You', *Wild Hope*

Day 15

Describe what you are grateful for right now, even if only in hindsight. Could you carry that into tomorrow?

Day 16

How easy do you find it to respect your boundaries?

Day 17

What do you notice about your habits? Have your
intentions begun to shape your movements?

Day 18

How could you welcome in more magic?

Day 19

When you are busy, how does your self-care fare?

Day 20

How is your inner voice? Is it kind/judgemental/defeatist?

Day 21

Do your thoughts run to worries and what-ifs when life is busy, or do you keep a fairly positive slant on your mindset?

Reflections

Let's use this space to visualise and manifest some moments of joy and magic ahead. If worrying is a waste of a good imagination, then let's put yours to better use. What would be welcome within your world? How could life embrace you better?

Your twinkly star-bright galaxy of *you*
is growing every day
reaching places that you haven't even been to
but your energy has
through your words or your actions.

From 'Your Beautiful Pathway', *I Wish I Knew*

Day 22

Spend some time bringing awareness to your body
and write about how it feels

Day 23

Write down five false things you have believed
about yourself

Day 24

Who do you admire right now and why? How could you
be inspired by their habits and ethos?

Day 25

How are your anger levels right now and what do you
do to process your anger when it appears?

Day 26

Write down five things you are grateful for

Day 27

How has your focus word helped shift your mindset recently?

Day 28

Has something been uncovered within you this month?
If so, describe it here

Day 29

This day is a bonus 24 hours to keep our calendar in tune
with the seasons and nature. What can you do with this
leap year day?

Reflections

As February comes to a close, take a moment to check in with yourself and your mindset. How would you describe your state of mind and your nervous system? How are your hope levels for the rest of the year and what are you looking forward to in the months ahead?

I'm a former pessimist, a recovering perfectionist, but I'm not aiming for optimism as you may think. I'm happy with realism, wrapped up in hope and sprinkled with some 'ah, but what if love really is the answer'.

From 'A Hopefulist', *Growing Brave*

FIRSTS

To see the 1st of each new month as the *first* is a powerful thing. A prompt from life reminding you that you are the author and if this story arc is not bringing you fulfilment, you can shape it as you see fit. A crisp, clean and excitingly blank fresh page. The next chapter. Full of hope, full of promise, full of more *living*. To see each 1st as a first is to invite in possibility and magic and, most of all, to reaffirm permission, power and possession. Follow the lead of the earth around you if you are unsure; are we rising, resting, regenerating, releasing, harvesting? Breathe into the flow. And off we go . . .

March

I believe words carry what they are and poetry is permission to infuse simple gatherings of letters with droplets of gold from the soul, which will stir up, create or release emotions from within the reader.

HELLO, MARCH

March, we meet again. I have long believed this month to be the harbinger of hope. If February is the springboard, a step up, then March is the launch pad – to new and to more. More life, more light, more time within our days and more space around us to let in more living. In the northern hemisphere, nature is calling us to awaken, and for me this is the perfect time to put some plans into action. March is filled with promise, and where there is promise and hope, magic is afoot. Look out for it this month. It is rising.

My word for the month is

I hope this word will allow me to

Day 1

What does March mean to you?

Day 2

How could your focus word help you this month?

Day 3

On a scale of one to ten, what level would you place your self-worth at?

Day 4

How are you different this month compared to last?

Day 5

What would you like to gently change about yourself
this month and why?

Day 6

What habits could you adopt to support your changes?

Day 7

What have you done for self-care recently?

Reflections

Use this space to express gratitude for what is here now and what you would love to welcome in as March unfolds. Do hope and excitement sneak their way through as you write? And if not, how can you make more space for it?

Sow seeds
wherever you go
there is nothing better you can do with your words
than plant a precious seed.

From 'Say It', *Life*

Day 8

Who are you grateful for within your world right now?

Day 9

What are you looking forward to and why?

Day 10

When you are most busy, how do you protect your self-care?

Day 11

Has your focus word created new happenings
so far this year?

Day 12

Think of a previous version of you. Do you love
yourself more now, or less?

Day 13

How does your life feel as a whole right now?

In what situations are you not yet using your focus word
to bring yourself into the present and recentre?

Reflections

I would suggest using this space to reach into your solar plexus and see what is there. What are you feeling right now? Which emotions are high today and which are throbbing silently, infusing your thoughts? Bring them all to the front, greet them and accept them as they are. Release the ones that do not serve you going forward.

Remember the smiles of the day
the laughter, the little wins
the warm words... and let
everything
else
go.

From 'When Your Head Hits the Pillow Tonight', *To the Women*

Day 15

Did joy sneak into your world recently? Write about it here

Day 16

How easy are you finding it to respect yourself?

Day 17

Which behavioural habits in others do you have least patience for?

Day 18

How does poor sleep affect your emotions?
Are you sleeping well?

Day 19

What brings you the most joy right now?

Day 20

When did sadness last visit?

Positive thinking happens only after accepting the negatives and processing. Agree or disagree?

Reflections

Let's use this space to list all the ways in which we are useful, helpful and kind on a daily basis. Leave nothing out – the smaller the better.

It is only when we are grown
that we truly see who *grew* us.

From 'One Day You Will See',
Growing Brave

Day 22

What situation are you struggling to process or cope with right now? How could you better face it?

Day 23

Write down five ways in which you are beautiful, from the point of view of your fiercest admirer

Day 24

Which parts of your day could you readjust to better
serve your peace and joy?

Day 25

How are you feeling about your place in the world/
your family/your life?

Day 26

Write down five things you are hoping for

Day 27

Write down five true things about your March so far

Day 28

Spend a little time thinking about the many versions
of you you've been

PROMPT: Can you name their decades/timelines; the curious one/the fearless one?

Let them argue
let them fight
let them believe
they are right

let them laugh
behind your back
they cannot push you
from your track

keep your focus
on the sky
and all the beauty
you pass by

but of all
you let them do
do not let them
alter you

let them lie
if they must
it's yourself
you need to trust.

From 'Let Them', *Wild Hope*

Day 29

How could you better accept and 'let them'?

Day 30

Write down three unkind things you have done recently

Day 31

How can you go ahead and rewrite the unkind ways you have acted out, to others or to yourself? Could you see this as an exciting mission to control your own narrative and put more kind energy out into the world?

Reflections

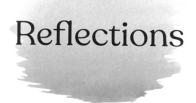

As March comes to a close, how do you feel? Are you unfurling with nature or still too exhausted to feel the light come in? If you are approaching autumn where you live, are you starting to hunker down? Wherever you are, always try to think of ways to rest. And on we go . . .

SPRING

I have always believed spring to be *the* harbinger of hope, the launch pad to lighter days, the gateway to life. Spring soothes our winter-worn souls with anticipation, and its promise of *more*. It gently shakes our hibernating toes and whispers, *wake now, your wintering days are done.* And so, with each eager sunrise, we emerge, we reignite, we re-energise. And as with the nature around us, we begin to rise and renew. Come on in, spring, we have much longed for your light, for your joy, for your *new*. We are slowly rousing from slumber, welcome back.

From *Wild Hope*

April

Somewhere inside you, there is a little firecracker
desperate to see more of this thing we call life
go get her, she's fun.

From 'Remember Her?', *To the Women*

WELCOME, APRIL

Welcome, spring (or autumn, depending on where you are in the world). Welcome, Mother Nature's bounty. As I open my arms to my second favourite month of the year, I also welcome in light. This month is my birthday month and has long signified joy for me. The weather is fresh and kinder than previous months, and there is a general feeling of creation and rebirth all around us. We are opening, unfurling, reaching and rising. It is exciting and inspiring; a great month to manifest much good.

My word for the month is

I hope this word will allow me to

Day 1

What does April feel like to you?

Day 2

How could your focus word shape this month?

Day 3

How honest do you think you are with yourself?

Day 4

How authentic would you say you are with others?

Day 5

What could you change to become more 'you' in daily life?

Day 6

What habits could you adopt to support your changes?

How kind is your inner voice right now and what
is it saying to intimidate you?

Reflections

April begins with Fools' Day, a day of light-hearted deceit in the name of fun, but I think it's a great time to reflect on ways we have been duped or tricked, by others or even by ourselves. Use this space to write about how this day makes you feel and how it affects your behaviour.

All this time you have wasted worrying you are not enough, when not only are you enough, you are more – more than you have ever been able to see and more than you can ever imagine possible.

From 'More', *I Wish I Knew*

Day 8

How have you shown up for yourself recently?

Day 9

What is on your gratitude list?

Day 10

How is April affecting your energy levels?

Day 11

Write down three mindful moments you could have today

Day 12

What is bringing disarray to your calm right now?

Day 13

What is letting in light for you?

How do you feel about yourself this month and is that different from last?

Reflections

Why not use this space to explore the honesty bond you have with yourself and how it is evolving. Is it tightening up or loosening? Are you able to call out old behaviour faster? How do you feel about truth within your own mental chatter?

So many versions of you exist
in very many places
but only you
will know the real one.

From `Only You`, *Love*

Day 15

In which ways does this world make honesty hard?

Day 16

What colour have your moods been this week?

Day 17

How are nature and the weather impacting you this month?

Day 18

Have you read any advice recently that has stuck with you?

Day 19

What is on your heart?

Day 20

Are you managing to stay mindful this month?

Write down three negative thoughts and
a perspective shift for each

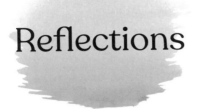

Reflections

As the seasons play out, do you feel yourself changing and evolving along with nature. Are you guided by the world outside?

What matters is how you live whilst you are here, how you respect this planet and those on it, how you love those gifted into your life and how you leave, having done as much of all of that as possible.

From 'Too Much', *Wild Hope*

Day 22

Write down five ways in which you are strong from the point of view of your fiercest admirer

Day 23

Which tasks do you daily face that affect your wellbeing?

Day 24

What is your biggest adversity right now and how can you better accept/cope with it?

Day 25

How did joy visit you recently and if not, is it possible
you may not have been open to it?

Day 26

Write down five true things about your April so far

What is true about your thought processes recently?
Have you perhaps been giving life to things that are not real?

Your life is a *lot*
the world is a *lot*
your mind is a *lot*
so today
this week
this year
why don't you take some time
to look at what you already do
and what an impressive machine
you actually are
you're a whole lot
(and that's more than enough).

From 'A Lot', *Life*

Day 28

Have you laughed enough this month?

Day 29

Write down three beautiful life truths

Day 30

What hopes and imaginings can you pin to the universe?
Which feelings and situations would you like to see more
of going forward, and which less?

Reflections

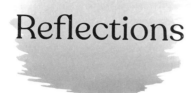

As April comes to a close, what is within your heart? Is there excitement and inspiration, or worry and dread? Are you feeling inspired by the seasons and their call to bloom?

MAY

May your days be filled with laughter
may your chores complete themselves
may your mind have time to wander
to a sandy beach of shells

may your morning stretch be graceful
may your lunch be full of taste
may your inspiration find you
may no moment go to waste

may your lonely days be lacking
may your friendships linger strong
may your thoughts be full of wonder
may your worries all be gone

may your money flow like water
may your problems float away
may your needs be met and more so
may you wake to sunny days

may you find the strength inside you
may you learn to look within
may you see yourself more kindly
may that journey now begin.

From 'May', *To the Women*

May

I hope there are days when the sun is warm, the breeze is on your skin and the laughter is loud. I hope you *live* sometimes and connect to the source of all that matters. And I hope today is that day. I really do.

From 'I Really Do', *Wild Hope*

COME ON IN, MAY

Welcome, May. In the northern hemisphere, May is green for go.
I feel the completion of a long-coming renewal in my bones, which
filters through to my movements. Energy is rising and more light
entices me onward. If your place of existence is nearing autumn's
end right now, you may feel the opposite entirely. Be led by nature,
always, and do as she does.

My word for the month is

I hope this word will allow me to

Day 1

What does May look like to you?

Day 2

How could your focus word shape this month?

Day 3

How is your energy?

Day 4

What colour are your emotions?

Day 5

What makes you feel most alive?

Day 6

How does writing in a journal help you embrace more life?

Day 7

How is your inner voice this week?
Is it calm and patient or anxious and critical?

Reflections

Write down as many ideas as you can about how you can bring the wisdom of this month's guiding word into next week. Can you think of one small thing you can do differently next week to help you focus on it?

Listen for the love in everything you hear today
it doesn't always sound like it should
but it's there
it's there.

From 'Listen for the Love', *Love*

Day 8

How are you sleeping and how is it affecting your emotions?

Day 9

What is on your gratitude list?

Day 10

How is the change of light affecting your energy
levels this month?

Day 11

Write down three things, big or small, that bring you joy

Day 12

What have you found hardest recently?

Day 13

How have you practised self-care this week?

Day 14

How do you feel about the month so far?
Does it feel different to last month?

Reflections

Why not use this space to explore your ideas, thoughts and feelings about journalling? Have you found it hard to do? Has it prompted you to change your mindset or your actions in any way?

I believe there is nothing that cannot be improved by taking the thoughts from your mind, the feelings from your heart, the signs from your soul and combining them together to create messages you need to read.

Day 15

Write about three things in nature that bring you
peace and serenity

Day 16

What colour has the sky been recently and how
has it affected your mood?

Day 17

What helps you feel calm? Can you create that?

Day 18

What has surprised you about journalling?

Day 19

What is on your mind?

Day 20

How has your guiding word helped you this month?

Write down three positive things about yourself and come back to read them again every day next week

MAY

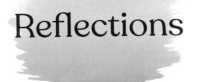

Reflections

Use this space to write a note to your younger self.
What do you wish you had known?

Stop telling the world all that you are not
and start showing them all that you *are*
expect that they will see the wonderful parts of you
because they will
if *you* do.

From 'Magically So', I Wish I Knew

Day 22

How kind to yourself have you been recently?

Day 23

What are you finding most difficult?

Day 24

What helps you remain focused when you have many
demands on your time and attention?

Day 25

How has beauty visited you lately and if not, is it possible
you may not have been open to it?

Day 26

Have you seen, heard or read anything today that inspired you?

Day 27

Write down five true things about your week

Day 28

What would you like to bring more attention to in your life?

Day 29

In which ways does this world make it hard to believe
in yourself?

Which people in your life see you as you are and love you
for yourself? Are you on that list?

Whatever you focus
your attention on
grows
so with this in mind
why not start ignoring
all the things
that bring you down
and start focusing instead
on the stuff that charges you up
from the inside out
things you truly *love*.

From `Attention', *Love*

Day 31

How could you make daily changes to be kinder to yourself?

Reflections

As we lay close to this month of May, what feelings are allowing you to align with nature and which are holding you back? Has your energy increased or waned? Can you lay down the things that weigh you here and leave them to the month of May? She will take them for you. Can you enter June free of that baggage? Let's try . . .

A DAY IS NOT LOST

A day is not lost
if you failed to tick off a list
or a diet was broken
a day is only lost
if you forgot
to say something kind
to yourself
or another
if you forgot
to pause
to search
for a tiny spark of beauty
amongst the drudgery
glimmering like gold
in the mud
a day is only lost
if you forgot
that life
even in the worst of times
is still a *gift*
a gift you so very much deserve
to *live* through
and not just **survive.**

From 'A Day is Not Lost', *Wild Hope*

June

Pray how can you say you have no chapters left
when the book that you're writing is hardly bereft
of adventures and lessons and stories you've woven
as you bravely embrace the choices you've chosen.

From 'On Time', *Growing Brave*

WELCOME IN, JUNE

Another new month, a fresh page – let us write on it together.
To me, June is the first sister of summer, or perhaps she is winter
for you. As we veer into the centre point of this year, it is natural to
feel a slight panic about time's passing. It is easy to feel we blinked
and missed. Let us both, then, use this moment to bring in our
awareness. Let us try to be *here* this month. Let us work on being
present and sharpening our vision.

My word for the month is

I hope this word will allow me to

165

Day 1

What does June feel like to you?

Day 2

How could your focus word shape this month?

Day 3

How are you feeling about the year so far?

Day 4

What has surprised you most about this year?

Day 5

What do you wish you could slow down more for this month?

Day 6

Where do you think you could be more present in your life?

Day 7

How could you create more space for what you love?

Reflections

Use this space to think about how the six guiding words you've chosen each month have helped you approach the year so far. What wisdom are they bringing you? Have they helped you see yourself better? Are there one or two that feel more natural than the rest?

I have found that life is everything
sometimes in one day
it is exhilarating
terrifying
joyful
heartbreaking.

From 'Life', *Life*

Day 8

How have you been creative recently?

Day 9

If today were a colour, what colour would it have been
for you and why?

Day 10

Look for beauty in something small today and write about it here

Day 11

What have you done for yourself this week?

Day 12

What have you found hardest about this month?

Day 13

Write down five things you are grateful for

Day 14

How is your inner voice this week?
Is it generally supportive or negative?

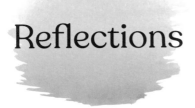

Reflections

Use this space to reflect on the passing of time. How could you do more of what is helpful for your wellbeing and less of what is unhelpful?

There is so much more of you yet
to discover in fact, that you
won't be done discovering *you*
for a very long time.

From 'More', I Wish I Knew

Day 15

Try to find three things around you that bring you joy

Day 16

What range of emotions have you been feeling?

Day 17

How have other people affected your mood?

Day 18

Think about your boundaries. How good are you at
looking after yours?

Day 19

How present have you been when listening to others this week?

Day 20

How present have you been when listening to yourself this week?

Day 21

We're around the midpoint of the year, how does this make you feel?

Reflections

Use this space to reflect on the midpoint of the year. What has gone well? What have you found hard? As you enter the second half of the year, what awareness can you bring from the first half to help you on your journey?

If you strive for something
anything
strive for truth
for peace
for kindness
for fun
for adventure
for joy
for wisdom
just be sure you don't strive to be like the crowd.

From 'If You Strive', *I Wish I Knew*

JUNE

183

Day 22

What are you striving for this week?

Fly high
dream big
live loudly
love fiercely
show the world
what you are made of, my love
show them your light
let it shine out there.

From `Home`, _Love_

Day 23

What would you like to bring more of into your life?

Day 24

What would you like to have less of in your life?

Day 25

How could you make more space for joy?

Day 26

Look for joy in small things. What have you found?

How is writing in a journal helping you think about yourself?

There is little we can do to control the world
but we can control our reaction to it
and we can remember
that everything is temporary
and anything can change in a heartbeat
so if peace is your aim
then be the peace you seek
when there is no peace to be found
you can bring it
you can *be* it.

From 'Be the Peace', *Life*

Day 28

Write down how you feel about control.
How much do you need it or seek it?

Day 29

Write down how you feel about letting go.
How easy or difficult do you find it?

Day 30

As the month comes to a close, write about how the ideas of being more present and letting go could help you approach the rest of the year

Reflections

As June slips away, how are you feeling about your life and yourself? Check in with your nervous system: is it on alert or autopilot? This is a wonderful time in the year's flow to see how the way you live affects your body and whether you could bring in more balance and calm, and create more space for grace.

JULY

We are halfway through this year. I know you wish you had done more. I know there are people you wish were still here. And I know that once again life has distracted you. But that's okay. This is exactly how it ebbs and flows. It is never easy. And the pain is often too much. But take a moment to readjust your vision. To remove the need for comparison and perfection. You are human. Life is messy but beautiful. You are messy and so beautiful. Arm yourself for the next half of the year with hope, love and quiet courage. No hard edges here. We know that true power comes through the soft, the warm and the willing. Arms wide open. Welcome, July . . .

July

Not seizing every day
like the gift that it is
is the biggest risk we take.

From 'Risk', *Wild Hope*

HELLO, JULY

Here we are, half way. Six months in and six months ahead.
Let us stop and breathe this beat together. Look at how you have
advanced this year already. And if flashes of regret or failure
abound, remind them you are human and life is all things. It is
not possible to predict your story in January, as we often believe
we can. You are in the flow of this life. All you can control is your
acceptance, your gratitude and your desire to manifest more
peace and abundance. We are *here*, what a thing. On we go . . .

My word for the month is

I hope this word will allow me to

Day 1

What does July mean to you?

Day 2

How could your focus word shape this month?

Day 3

How are your energy levels?

Day 4

What is your biggest achievement so far this year?

Day 5

Have you been kind to yourself lately? How so?

Day 6

How are you feeling?
What effect is it having on your levels of peace?

Day 7

Pause and slow your breathing to create a few minutes of calm.
Write about how it feels and any obstacles you encounter

JULY

Reflections

Use this space to reflect on a recent disappointment. It can be something small or something big. Try to be kind to yourself and consider how you could shift that perspective and see the positives. If there are none, write about that . . .

You can't be sure
what's in store for you
on this journey
but you can decide
that you won't be broken
in the same way twice.

From 'And You Can', Life

Day 8

How is your inner voice? Is it supporting you?

Day 9

How is the weather affecting your mood?

Day 10

If today were a colour, what colour would it be and why?

Day 11

What has gone well recently and what has brought
out negative habits?

Day 12

How is your guiding word helping you through this month?

Day 13

Write down five things you are grateful for this week

Day 14

What are you most excited about in your life right now?

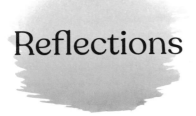

Reflections

Use this space to write a letter to your inner voice. What could it do more or less of? How could it be more kind and patient? Where do you think this voice came from?

Make some time to accept all that you are – the messy, the raw, the loud and the joyous – and then go out there and take up some space without apologising for the realness you leave in your wake.

From 'Unleash', *Wild Hope*

Day 15

Think of three things in nature that bring you joy
and write them down

Day 16

How does respecting your boundaries make you feel?

Day 17

Who have you been missing?

Day 18

How are you feeling about yourself?

JULY

Day 19

How tired are you feeling?

Day 20

What has made you unhappy recently?

Day 21

Write about someone or something that makes you feel
angry or passionate, and why

Reflections

Spend time thinking about forgiveness. Is there someone you need to or would like to forgive? If not, why? Could you write a creative verse about what forgiveness is and why it matters?

PROMPT: What colour is forgiveness? How would it look in nature? What does it sound like?

When your head hits the pillow tonight, my friend, close your eyes and remember, you are worthy.

From 'When Your Head Hits the Pillow Tonight', To the Women

Day 22

Write down three kind things you have done or seen
this month

Speak up
say the words
do the *stuff*
ride the waves
head down through the storms
accept the dark
the light will follow.

From 'Risk', *Wild Hope*

Day 23

How are your patience levels this week?

Day 24

Have you practised self-care recently?

Day 25

How are you feeling this week?

Day 26

How helpful do you find it writing in your journal?

Day 27

What fills you with positive energy?

Day 28

What have you noticed about nature this month?

JULY

Let life mould you
as you were meant to be
so different
so individual
no other exactly the same
because what art would be revered
if it was everywhere
identical?
be your own work in progress
you're a masterpiece in the making.

From 'Blank', *I Wish I Knew*

Day 29

What have you been most pleased about recently?

Day 30

What are you finding hard?

Day 31

Write about where you find support and kindness in your
life and where you would like to see more of this

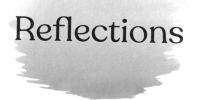

Reflections

As July comes to a close, use this space to reflect on what you are grateful for in the flow of this year and how this can help you approach the coming months.

SUMMER

Summertime, when the living is easy. When life is at
its bountiful peak and days are so deliciously long,
there is no end to the promise they hold. Summer
is the time to be alive, to make hay while the sun
shines and to fill your energy stores with memories
of joy, which will fill the otherwise empty hearths
of your heart with fire, all winter long. Do not let
worries or fears stop you from embracing the sun,
the *joy*, you so deserve, my friends. You are gifted
many summers in your life, but never quite enough.
You deserve to *live* them. To feel them. Summertime,
when the living is easy, so live *easy*.

From *Wild Hope*

August

You have done so much more than you realise. You're trailing a bright pathway that you don't even know about.

From 'You', *Wild Hope*

AND SO WE ROLL INTO AUGUST

I hope your heart is full and your cup runneth over. If you are finding this year hard, let August be a time when you pour more goodness into yourself. This month, to me, is the most spacious. It feels as if we can manipulate time to be on our side somehow. If this feels true to you, be sure to make it so. You must live, my friends, with intent. It is there for the taking but it won't come to you.

My word for the month is

I hope this word will allow me to

225

Day 1

What does August mean to you?

Day 2

How could your focus word shape this month?

Day 3

Does your heart feel full or empty?

Day 4

What has been your most joyful moment of the year so far?

Day 5

What have you been finding challenging this year?

Day 6

If you had all the time in the world today, what would you do with it?

Day 7

Write about one thing you'd like to bring into your life this
month and set your intention to make it happen

Reflections

Use this space to reflect on what you are grateful for today. If life is hard right now, look for small things to help light up the dark.

Love what you have and you'll have what you love
it's the way to a life
full of pleasure
be kind to your life and your life will be kind
look around
you're surrounded by treasure.

From 'Surrounded by Treasure', *Wild Hope*

Day 8

What is opening up for you?

Day 9

How sharp has your focus been recently?

Day 10

Have you noticed anything different or shifting?

Day 11

What is on your gratitude list?

Day 12

How could your guiding word help your focus?

Day 13

Write about something you could do differently and something you can congratulate yourself on

Day 14

Has setting intentions changed you or your mindset at all?

Reflections

Use this space to write about what would help your heart feel fuller and lighter. What could you do more or less of to pour more goodness into yourself?

I hope you know the impact that you have today
I hope you see your light for what it is
I hope you do not pick yourself apart today
I hope you know this life is yours to live

From 'Today, I Hope', *Wild Hope*

Day 15

What do you feel hopeful about?

Day 16

How does nature bring lightness to your heart?

Day 17

How are your energy levels?

Day 18

How are you feeling about yourself?

Day 19

Write about something that has changed for you this year

Day 20

What has been your best moment recently?

Day 21

Write about how this week has been different to last week

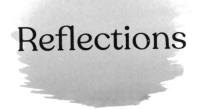

Reflections

Write about how it makes you feel when the sun shines on your skin and warms your body and mind.

If you wonder why you wane with the
moon and take power from the sun,
it is because you are one.

From `One`, *Life*

Day 22

How well have you been listening to your intuition recently?

You may not know
where you will end up
but something deep inside
tells you
it will be exactly where
you're supposed to be.

From 'And You Can', *Life*

Day 23

What is on your mind?

Day 24

Have you noticed any acts of kindness this week?

Day 25

How positive is your thinking right now?

Day 26

How does writing in your journal help with your mindset?

Day 27

How are your patience levels?

Day 28

How much support are you getting from your inner voice?

JUST A DAY

No, today probably won't be a great day, but it
absolutely won't be a bad day either. Today will
simply be a day. Twenty-four hours of a little bit
of everything. Some moments will be hard, some
will be joyous, some will be peaceful and some
will be draining. And you, you will handle it all,
because that's what you *do*. Don't put pressure
on yourself to have any kind of a day, my friend.
Life throws enough at you. Instead, just remind
yourself that whatever happens, you are ready.
And most importantly, you have your own back.
It's just a day. Another day of life in all its messy
everything-ness. **Lucky us.**

From *Wild Hope*

Day 29

What is the most beautiful thing you've seen recently?

Day 30

How are your self-acceptance levels this week?

Day 31

Today is the last day of August. Write about what has
changed for you this month

Reflections

As August comes to a close, use this space to reflect on all the ways you are enough just as you are. Think about how you have so much to give, both to yourself and to those who matter most to you.

HAVE THE COURAGE

Have the vision
to share your own story
the ugly truth heals
as much as the glory
pass down your lessons
the joy and the pain
remind those who follow
to dance in the rain.

From 'Have the Courage', *To the Women*

September

You don't meet anyone in this life
by accident
each person brings with them
a *joy*
a *love*
or a *lesson*
pay attention.

From 'You Don't Meet Anyone by Accident', *Wild Hope*

HELLO, SEPTEMBER

We meet again. We welcome you in with acceptance of nature's cycle and a release to the flow. If summer is waning where you are, she will silently remind you to seize each sunbeam and stockpile the gentle warmth, to fuel your lamps going forward. Do not miss a moment of her light. Take it in, take it all in. If the daily grind is increasing for you, be aware, balance is key. It can wait, but the last gasps of summer cannot.

My word for the month is

I hope this word will allow me to

Day 1

What does September mean to you?

Day 2

How could your focus word shape this month?

Day 3

Who has inspired you recently and why?

Day 4

How balanced is your equilibrium this week?

Day 5

Reflect on your connections with others and what they bring

Day 6

Try being present when you are doing something small and ordinary. Write about what appears

Try to spend time with someone important to you and be as present for them as you can. Write about how you savour those precious minutes together

Reflections

Use this space to write about what happens when you slow down and take root within the moment, either with people or in everyday activity. Does it make you feel more balanced and alive or more anxious and impatient?

I hope you see the beauty in the bland today
I hope you laugh until those tears just flow
I hope you let your soul be as it must today
I hope you'll finally learn to let it go.

From 'Today, I Hope', *Wild Hope*

Day 8

Take time to be still and do nothing.
What do you notice about your thoughts and body?

Day 9

What is on your gratitude list?

Day 10

How has your focus word helped you this week?

Day 11

Write about any changes in nature or light you have noticed

Day 12

How easy has it been to be patient lately?

Day 13

What is worrying you most?

How busy have you been this week and what impact
has it had on your wellbeing?

Reflections

We all have to-do lists. Use this space to write yourself a 'to-don't' list of things that aren't helping you, things you'd like to leave behind.

Wait up for the moon sometimes
or get up early to see a sunrise
just because you can
jump in the lake
run, skip, dance
the things you need to feel alive
are all around
you just have to see them.

From 'This Is No Waiting Room', *Life*

Day 15

How does your day-to-day life make being present hard?

Day 16

Is there anything you could action on your 'to-don't' list,
if only for one day?

Day 17

How are nature and the weather impacting you this week?

Day 18

What is on your mind?

Day 19

What feels different this month compared to last?

Day 20

How is your self-worth?

Day 21

Write down five things that help bring meaning to your life

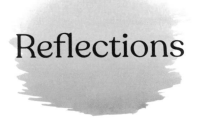

Reflections

Write down three things you would like to bring more of into your week next week. How can you make space for these?

You're writing a letter to the stars, each time you imagine something good. Manifesting *magic*. Be careful what you wish for, my friends. Wish wisely.

From 'Wish Wisely', *Wild Hope*

Day 22

How do you watch out for signs of overwhelm?

When your brain holds too much chaos, *sit down*. Take one thought at a time, look at it, spin it with your actual inner voice and not your inner critic, and place it gently where it should be.

From 'Do Less', *Wild Hope*

Day 23

What has been your biggest adversity recently?

Day 24

When did joy last visit you and, if not, is it possible you
may not have been open to it?

Day 25

Has your focus word helped shift your mindset recently?

Day 26

Write down five ways you are brave, from the point of view of your fiercest supporter

Day 27

What have you noticed about the times you've been present this month? Have they shifted your perspective at all?

I looked back
and didn't see
my failures
my flaws
or my
not being enough-ness

I didn't see
wrinkles
cellulite
or numbers on scales

I didn't see
cars
possessions
or money made

I looked back
and saw
a life
lived to the full.

From 'I Looked Back', *Wild Hope*

Day 28

Write down three things September has brought you

Day 29

How are you feeling about your place in the world/
your family/your life?

Day 30

What are you looking forward to next month and why?

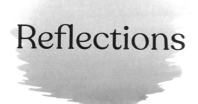

Reflections

As September comes to a close and a new season comes into view, what is within your heart? How does your life feel as a whole right now?

AUTUMN

Most rejoice at the sight of spring, but I have always
loved autumn. Rich, righteous colours, a shedding of
weight and submission to a force larger than you.
The revelation of one's true self. Bare and unafraid.
Warmed and dressed not by folly, but by innate
wisdom. And the *knowing*, that this is as it must be
and *everything will pass*. Autumn does not shudder
at the thought of winter ahead; it peacefully basks
in the last of the sun, counting every moment as
a blessing and a vital part of the journey. It lets its
leaves fall to the ground to nurture the new, like
droplets of nourishing gold, and finds peace where
no peace existed before. I've always loved autumn.
It's the letting go, you see. Let it *go*.

From *Wild Hope*

October

Beautiful moments are everywhere,
waiting to be seen.

From `Magic´, *Wild Hope*

OCTOBER ARRIVES

If autumn is in full flourish in your world, watch and learn. Let go. Let old leaves fall away and do not be afraid to bare all. New life returns, everything is temporary and holding on too tight strangles the flow, like a foot on a hose pipe. Walk out of old clothes. Walk bare into the new. Throw out the ideas that suffocate you and embrace the naked truth. You are not afraid to be cold; light warms from within. Shake off. Stand tall. Welcome what's ahead.

My word for the month is

I hope this word will allow me to

Day 1

What does October mean to you?

Day 2

How could your focus word shape this month?

Day 3

What are you feeling grateful for?

Day 4

What seasonal changes have you noticed recently?

Day 5

Choose one simple thing you could do more or less of this month to bring more calm into your days. Write down how you will make this happen

Day 6

What have you noticed about trying to change your one thing. Has anything surprised you?

Day 7

Write about a truth you have discovered about yourself this year

Reflections

Use this space to reflect on what you are ready to let go of, big or small, in your life and/or your thinking. How could you allow these things to fall away? Choose one or two to focus on next week.

And as with everything
everything
in life
change is constant
and nothing stays the same.

From `For a Lifetime`, *Love*

Day 8

How well do you generally deal with change?

Day 9

Write about why it is sometimes hard to let go

Day 10

Have you noticed anything shifting as you bring
awareness in?

Day 11

What three words describe change for you?

Day 12

How can your guiding word help you release what is no
longer serving you?

Day 13

How has your intent around releasing and letting go shifted
your thinking this week?

Day 14

When we let go of things we no longer need, we create space for the new. Write about something new you would like to invite into your life

Reflections

Use this space to write about what has shifted inside you recently. Look back on this month or further back to the start of the year. Does anything feel different? What would you like to invite more of into your life? Or have any particular events changed your outlook?

You won't get your share of the good stuff if you're carrying yesterday's rubbish. See each new dawn as a chance to be free of the past. New page, clean slate, hands free.

From 'Yesterday's Rubbish', *Wild Hope*

Day 15

What first steps could you take towards inviting
something new into your life?

Day 16

How are you feeling about change?

Day 17

Write about one small thing you've done differently.
How did it go?

Day 18

What have you noticed about the light outside?

Day 19

How truthful have you been with yourself recently?
Could you be kinder?

Day 20

Write down three beautiful truths about yourself from
the point of view of your fiercest admirer

Day 21

What have you noticed about your inner voice this week?
Has it been truthful or unhelpful? What does it say to you
when you think about change?

Reflections

Use this space to write a short letter of thanks to some part of you or your life you'd like to change or let go of. Explain why it's time to part ways and wish it well on its journey without you.

Standing at the edge of a new chapter can be scary. The desire to run back into the pages you know so well is more than tempting. But you must keep moving. Chapters end, even the good ones. And if you linger in the past too long, your story cannot unfold the way it should.

From 'The Edge', *Wild Hope*

Day 22

How can you take some time to reignite or keep bright your *spark*?

When you take the first tentative steps
back out there
you'll resurface
your spark will reignite
lightly at first
but then brighter than ever before.

From 'Numb', *Life*

Day 23

How are your energy levels?

Day 24

How busy have you been this month and how did
this affect you?

Day 25

How is your guiding word helping you?

Day 26

Write about something beautiful you've seen recently

Day 27

In what way would you like to be more brave?

Day 28

Encourage your inner voice to be supportive of you.
Write about what happens

You are not a witch, my friend
you are quite simply
or *complicatedly*
a woman

and your magic is not something
you can choose, or lose
it always is
and always has
lived within you

and you need no longer hide it

they call it the witch wound
but the time to heal is here
now
let that magic out.

From 'The Witch Wound', *Wild Hope*

Day 29

What do you think your 'witch wound' might be?

Day 30

As Hallowe'en approaches, what magic within you
can you let out?

Day 31

Write about ways in which your thinking/behaviour could
be seen as magical . . .

Reflections

As we greet October's end, how are you feeling? Take a moment to check in with your inner self and see if the monologue is critical or kind. Are you balancing busy with breath or have things become less centred and more chaotic? Check in, release what is not serving you and be free of it, ready to greet another clean page of your book with fresh eyes. Let old leaves fall away . . .

YOU'LL BE OKAY

The one thing we know for sure, is that nothing lasts
for ever. In this journey, you will grieve. You will grieve
people who are still alive, as well as those who have
passed on. You will grieve shattered dreams, and you
will grieve versions of yourself you had to break free
from. But that's okay. In this life nothing lasts for ever
but with that same truth comes the knowledge that
all pain will dissipate too. And great new things will
emerge. Wonderful new people who shine light into
your soul will come on in, if you leave space. And as
long as you cry when you must, laugh when you can
and love every day your little broken heart still beats,
you will be okay. You will be more than okay.

From *Growing Brave*

November

We are not alone, and we are never without support. Don't fear the long nights, my friend, look to the skies for reassurance, that light always comes back. The sun and the moon, they *have* us. And they work together, diligently, to ensure we go on. So *go on*.

From 'They Have Us', *Wild Hope*

NOVEMBER

To me, November has aways felt like the first sister of winter.
Perhaps she is summer to you? Either way, this month can often
be missed in preparation for the colourful carousel of Christmas
ahead. If your world is losing light right now, bring it in, create it.
Replace what nature removes with the optimism she inspires. Find
it within you and make it real. There is light to be found all around, if
you are open to see it.

My word for the month is

I hope this word will allow me to

Day 1

What does November mean to you?

Day 2

How could your focus word shape this month?

Day 3

How could you slow down more this month?

Day 4

What makes you feel most tired?

Day 5

Where do you look for light?

Day 6

Where have you found rest this week?

Day 7

Has sadness visited you recently?
What was it trying to tell you?

Reflections

Use this space to think about why nature rests in winter. How could you bring more rest into your day-to-day as you approach the end of the year?

Pay attention to the voices in your head
not all of them are on your side
some sneaked in the back door
when the world first broke your heart
and found a place to stay.

Adapted from *I Wish I Knew*

Day 8

When was the last time you felt anxious and why?

Day 9

What age do you see your inner child as and why?

Day 10

What are your worst childish behaviours and where do
you think they stem from?

Day 11

What are your worst grown-up behaviours and where do
you think they stem from?

Day 12

What are your best childlike behaviours and how have you
managed to retain them?

Day 13

Write down a piece of advice you'd like to give to your inner child

Day 14

Describe the feelings that connecting with your inner child
has brought up

Reflections

Use this space to reflect on memories that may have resurfaced recently and how they can affect your current perspective on the world around you and the life you have built.

I think it's really vital that you remember the sun still shines. No matter how thick the cloud, no matter how many days it's been since you last felt those rays. They are there. Battling to reach you, battling to warm the soil and radiate life.

From 'The Sun', *Wild Hope*

Day 15

Write about something around you that brings you joy

Day 16

What piece of advice would you give your 16-year-old self?

Day 17

What would your 16-year-old self think of you
and your life now?

Day 18

In which ways could you include your inner child or
teenager more?

Day 19

How present have you been for yourself this week?

Day 20

If you judged your inner voice on its friendship qualities,
how would it come out?

Day 21

Do you think it's important to accept and include the old versions of you within your self-love practices? What could this achieve for the 'you' you are today?

Reflections

Use this space to describe your inner voice and how its support or adversity fluctuates depending on your levels of stress and busyness. Does it create the stress, or simply react, or both?

Pay attention to the voices in your head
not all of them are on your side
some sneaked in the back door
when the world first broke your heart
and found a place to stay.

Adapted from, *I Wish I Knew*

Day 22

How have you been brave recently?

Day 23

In which ways could you be more brave to create a more joyful life?

Day 24

How is your fear holding you back right now?

You might just miss the most beautiful moments
of your life, whilst grieving the ones gone by.
It's scary at the edge, my friend, I know.
But just jump. You have so much ahead. And the
good stuff behind, will always be there.

From 'The Edge', *Wild Hope*

Day 25

What fears have you picked up within the last year that
you didn't have before?

Day 26

Have you become more or less fearful in recent years?
Why do you think that is?

Day 27

How is writing in a journal helping you think about yourself?

HOW YOU GROW

The bravest thing you can do
is be kind to yourself
when you feel
you deserve it
the *least*
when you are imperfect
when you have failed
when you are off track
out of whack
and flawed
if you can find
that grain of kindness
for your most unloveable self
it will land
like blessed raindrops
on a parched plant
and that, my friend
is how you grow.

From *Love*

Day 28

How do you feel about control?
How much do you need it or seek it?

Day 29

How easy or difficult do you find going with the flow?

Day 30

How could the idea of being more present and letting go
help you approach the rest of the year?

Reflections

As November comes to a close, use this space to stitch some gratitude to the fabric of the universe and set some intentions for December. What are you seeking? Imagine it is here already and be grateful in advance. This is manifesting . . .

DECEMBER

December, please be kind
to those who find your light too bright
let them see that hope lives
in every card, every invitation
and every glass raised
and for gifts
bring them memories old and new
and show them what to do
with all that love.

December

Let them put up their lights
let them decorate their trees
and fill their souls
they are fighting their own fight
in the loveliest of ways.

From 'Let Them Put Up Their Lights'

COME ON IN, DECEMBER

December, come on in with your lights, your music and your promise of joy. Let your festive graces warm our hardened hearts and remind us of what is important. Fuse people together with your goodwill once more and be gentle to those who cannot accept your effusive joy, so deeply numbing is their pain. December, we embrace your joyful soul wholeheartedly, knowing we can rest our social selves in January.

My word for the month is

I hope this word will allow me to

Day 1

What does December mean to you?

Day 2

How could your focus word shape this month?

Day 3

How organised is your mind right now?

Day 4

How are you planning to maintain your energy
levels this month?

Day 5

Are you placing extra pressure on yourself right now?

Day 6

How can you take time out to recoup today and how does that feel?

Perfection could be banished this month and replaced with connection. Use this space to explore ways in which you can do this

Reflections

Use this space to write about what December and the festive season mean to you, depending on where you live and what you celebrate, and how you can better honour their core of peace and goodwill.

They say happiness is a choice, but I think it's
peace that we can choose, peace in the acceptance
that life is *everything*. And that's okay.

From `Happy', *Wild Hope*

Day 8

Write a card or send a message that crosses a bridge somehow. What does it bring up for you?

Day 9

What have you forgotten to give gratitude for?

Day 10

How has your focus word helped you remain in the flow?

Day 11

Write about how your nervous system feels right now

Day 12

How is your inner voice? Is it kind or critical?

Day 13

What worries are you holding on to that could be
relegated to the universe?

Day 14

Is your level of peace balanced with your level of busy?
How could you change that for the better?

Reflections

Make a list of ways you will find calm and balance this month and pin them to the fabric of the universe to be upheld.

If you cannot bear the music
or find the energy to be merry and bright
that's okay
just make it through until next year
one day at a time
hang on in
you are loved.

Day 15

Are you letting yourself go to joy when it arrives?

Day 16

Is there something you could do to bring calm to your core?

Day 17

How do you differentiate between people-pleasing
and kindness (remembering that you are people too)?

Day 18

What is on your heart?

Day 19

What feels different this month compared to last?

Day 20

How is your self-worth?

Day 21

Write down five ways you can open up to light

Day 22

What could you do to bring more of what you want
into this week?

You forgot the gravy because you were busy being
present and drinking in the joy of connection.
That's where the love lives...

Adapted from 'Forgotten Gravy', *Wild Hope*

Day 23

How are your energy levels? Are you practising self-care?

Day 24

How has sadness visited you this week and has she been with you more than you would have liked in the past few months?

Day 25

Write down three ways December has filled your soul

Day 26

What have you noticed about your self-worth levels this year?

Day 27

Write down five ways you've changed this year

Day 28

What has been your biggest achievement this year?

A FOCUS WORD REFLECTION...

Use this space to make a note of all the guiding words you have used for each month. How have they helped your mindset this year?

January	July
February	August
March	September
April	October
May	November
June	December

Day 29

How are you feeling about your journalling practice this year?
Has it been helpful?

What five words describe this year for you?

I hope you like the way your story goes today
I hope you see the hero there is you
I hope you'll write the chapter you deserve today
I hope the happy ending will come true

Adapted from 'Today, I Hope', *Wild Hope*

Reflections

As this year careers to a close, reflect on the version of you that exists right now. Are you changing again, as we move into another turn around the sun? Remember, you are enough, more than enough, and be sure to tell any old versions of you exactly that.

I think every version of the person we have been lives within us still, like those wooden nesting dolls we played with as children. And truly, we cannot begin to fully love ourselves until we take each one of those dolls out and honour them, just as they are. They were exactly who they were, so that you could be you today. And each is so beautiful.

Adapted from 'Nesting Dolls', *Growing Brave*

Day 31

Which practices and habits are you looking to bring
with you into next year and why?

WINTERING

You may think yourself lazy, or flawed. Yet your body is made of almost exactly the same elements as the stars. Your bone composition matches perfectly the coral in the seas, and you, my friend, are ruled by the moon and the sun, the tides and the planets. Whether you like it or not. So, no, you are not *lazy*, you are not *late*. Nature is simply pulling you to slow, like the life, flora and fauna around you. It is not your moment to rise. Look around you. It is winter. You are *wintering*. And you are right on time.

From *Wild Hope*

LETTING GO

Please use this space to leave behind any thoughts, fears or habits that are holding you back. Write a letter to the year we are leaving and ask it to keep those things for you. I hope this is as powerful for you as it has been for me. We move ahead, much lighter.

YOU JUST GREW

It is brave to want to be better
and braver still to understand
that you are already enough
but reaching for more is your right
you are a seed instructed by light
not a creature of the night
and if the other flowers in your field
do not support the way you grow
let them go
all they need to know
is that you are courageous
to want new
you are nature
you just grew
and that's okay
you did not come here to stay
let old leaves
    fall
     away.

From *Growing Brave*

Final word

Thank you for journalling with me here this year; what a thing we have shared. It matters not if you were consistent or dedicated, but I hope the habit of big-picture thinking (to sharpen focus in the moment) brought some interesting perspectives your way. I will be hosting a live session to discuss this with you all, so do look out for that on my social media pages.

Keep this journal as a point of reference for the months and years ahead; it is wonderful to see how our growth expands our thought processes and behaviours. We are always growing, never still. Even when you feel completely stuck, it's likely a cocoon, not a cage. Keep reaching for light; petals to the sun . . . and on we grow.

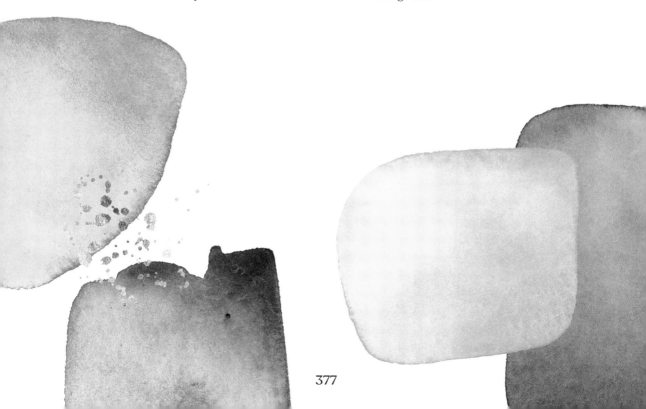

DEAR JOURNALLER,

I would love for you to take this space and create a poem of your choice. Any subject matter, any style. All you have to do to get in the poetry writing zone is to switch off your thinking and engage your feelings/soul. The message and the atmosphere of emotion is the key. If you are feeling empowered, we will share these with one another.* I would like that very much indeed.

*Details of how you can share these are on my website

About the author

Donna Ashworth is a No. 1 *Sunday Times* bestselling poet. She lives in the hills of Scotland with her husband, two sons, Brian and Dave (the dogs) and Sheldon (the cat).

Donna started her social media accounts in 2018 in a bid to create a safe social space for women to come together and connect, but her love of all things wordy quickly became the focus and a past love for poetry was reignited. Over nine books and 1.8 million followers later, Donna is delighted daily with her mission to shower the world with words and make poetry a go-to in our wellbeing toolkit.

'I believe wholeheartedly in the power of opening a daily poetry page to better everyone's mental health and clear space within our minds. Poetry is permission to feel everything we as humans are absolutely supposed to, knowing we are not alone, never alone. Poetry is not folly for the fancy; it is using words to shift perspectives, heal wounds and let in light again. And it is something we can pass to one another when times become turbulent, as they so often will.'

Facebook @DonnaAshworth
Instagram @DonnaAshworthWords
TikTok @DonnaAshworthWordy
X/Twitter @Donna_ashworth
www.donnaashworth.com

'A word to you
you are
without doubt
needed
but rarely *seen*
perhaps seeing yourself
here
will be a step to saying
thank you
vertebra by vertebra
you are magnificent.'

From `Backbones', *Wild Hope*

Acknowledgements

Thank you to all my followers who join with me annually at the start of a new turn around the sun. Thank you for allowing me to allocate focus words your way and to watch how the year unfolds with those thoughts at the forefront. And thank you for making this entire undertaking so much fun! Journalling really is a wonderful mental-health-mindset-exercise routine . . . and, as with all forms of exercise, the fun makes it flow so much more joyfully.

Thank you to Susanna, my editor, for her tireless attention to detail and thank you to lovely Leonie who cast her eagle eyes over this book to ensure the flow was as I intended. Thank you to Nick and Will at Bonnier Books for reworking the cover until my vision appeared and thank you to all the team who helped me manage this busy timeline and realise the dreams within my head. A big thank you too to Studio Nic&Lou for the beautifully designed pages of this journal.

Thanks to each and every person I have met within the last year who has shared their story with me so I may pour their lessons and perspectives into my own writing flow. Together we make something beautifully useful. Day-to-day manuals for living well within our own minds and bodies. Quite the thing.

If you've enjoyed your journey with Donna
this year, you may also enjoy . . .

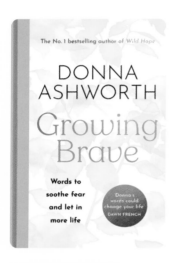

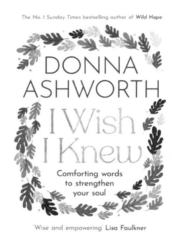

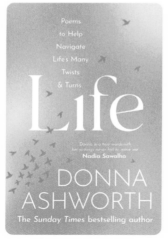

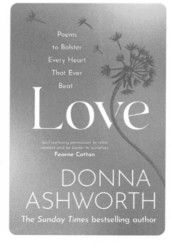

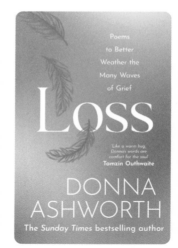